LET'S START
RIVER COARSE
FISHING

Richard Willett

The Crowood Press

First published in 1990 by
The Crowood Press
Ramsbury, Marlborough,
Wiltshire SN8 2HE

British Library Cataloguing in Publication Data

Willett, Richard
  River coarse fishing.
  1. Coarse fish. Angling. Manuals
  I. Title
  799.1'1

  ISBN 1–85223–307–9

Typeset by Jahweh Associates, Stroud
Printed in Great Britain by MacLehose & Partners Ltd

Contents

Fish and Location

Roach A very common fish to be found in rivers. The eye is red and there are tinges of red on the lower fins. The general body colouring is silver, but a specimen roach may be brassy in colour.

Dace More streamlined than a roach and favours fast water. The eye is yellow; the edge of the anal fin is concave.

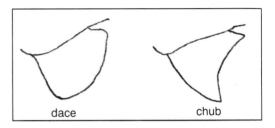
dace   chub

Chub The anal fin is convex – a means of identifying it from the dace. The chub favours stretches of river with plenty of cover.

Perch A handsome fish with a row of spines along the dorsal fin and some on its gill covers. The body is green; the anal and pelvic fins are a bright red.

Barbel A powerful fish that is found in fast-running stretches. Favoured haunts are weir pools and beneath undercut banks.

Bream One of the most popular fish with anglers, bream are bottom feeders and when a massive shoal of fish are feeding they can cause the water to become discoloured. Bronze bream can be large, and fish over fifteen pounds have been caught. Small bronze bream are called skimmers.

Gudgeon The gudgeon is often the first fish a young angler catches. They seldom grow larger than four ounces but for their size they are enjoyable to

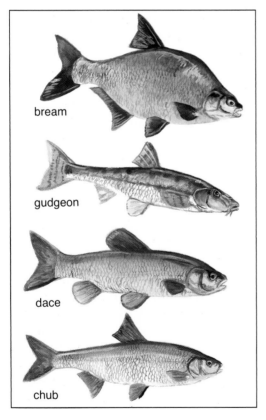
bream

gudgeon

dace

chub

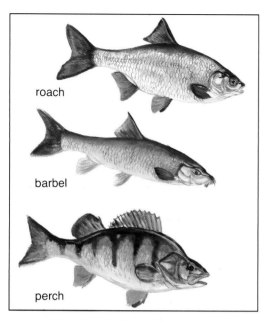

roach

barbel

perch

catch. Gudgeon are bottom feeders and shoal fish. They thrive where the river bed is gravelly and here they can be caught in large numbers.

GLIDES
Of all kinds of river swim, glides are probably the most predictable. In the typical glide, the current is medium paced, the depth is uniform, and in wind-free conditions the surface of the water is smooth with no sign of boiling or turbulence. Such swims occur on slower stretches of faster rivers.

Glides come in all shapes and sizes, depending on the dimension of the river in question. Depth can vary between three and ten feet.

A wide variety of plant and animal life inhabits glides, supplying a natural larder for fish. Milfoil, mare's-tail, dropwort and water buttercup are common, and in turn provide natural food such as bloodworm and snails. This is why most species of coarse fish prefer this type of habitat. Chub, roach and barbel in particular frequent glides. In summer, look for a glide close to your own bank that is arched over with bank-side undergrowth, trees or bushes – such swims are ideal.

Another attraction of glides is the number of fish present in them, especially large ones. Whether a glide is in a large or small river, it is likely to be more productive than other smaller pockets of water. Glides are natural shoaling areas and can provide several fish in one session. Fishing a glide on a big river takes time; do not keep changing swims. On small streams, however, you will be able to cover two or three glides in a day's roving.

RAPIDS AND WEIR POOLS
To many anglers, rapids conjure up visions of turbulent, foam-crested waters rushing over large boulders. These swims can be ideal places for big chub and dace. Weir pools, with their distinctive smell of wet weed and wild plants, are ideal for most species of fish. The illustration on pages 8 and 9 shows which currents attract individual species and where to place your bait. As weir pools can be dangerous places to fish, be very careful.

streamer weed

silt bottom

fresh

bloodworm

gravel bot

Glide.

willows

sluice gate

back eddy

turbulent run, 12–14ft deep

even glide, about 50ft long, 9–10ft deep

hrimp

streamer weed

fly larvae

barbel

cast in and let bait drift

dace

roach

barbel

Weir pool.

8

main weir

head of weir – good place to put a bait

roach

perch

chub

9

Trotting Basics

When trotting a float, the bait and the float are allowed to travel down a section of river at the pace of the current. Before beginning to fish, the actual depth of the swim should be established.

This can easily be done without having to use a plummet. Set the float to the depth you imagine the swim to be. Cast out to where you intend to trot the bait down with the current and let the flow of the river carry the float downstream. Adjust the float up the line until the float drags under. This will happen when the hook begins to catch the river bed.

Once you have found the right depth you can set about catching some fish. Throw some loose feed, either in the form of maggots or casters, into the line

of the current in which you intend to trot your tackle. This will hopefully attract fish into the area. Don't throw in great balls of groundbait. Adopt a little-and-often process, with loose feed being thrown in every other cast.

Cast out into the head of your swim and leave the bail arm open. As the current takes your float downstream start to control the speed of the float as it travels. Do this by applying gentle pressure with your forefinger on the line as it leaves the reel's spool. Hold the rod fairly high so that as little line as possible is in contact with the water's surface.

Begin by trotting with the bait touching the river bed, and if the fish begin to move up to feed, possibly intercepting your loose feed, you can

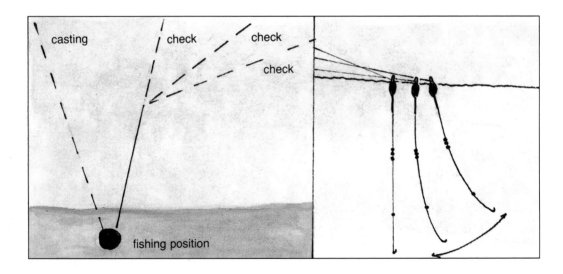

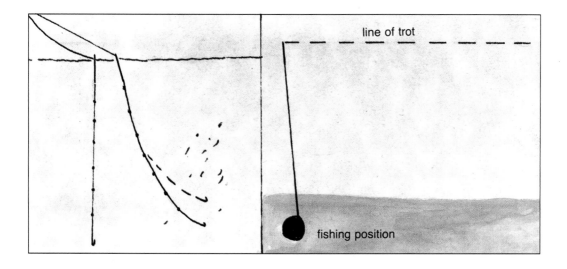

line of trot

fishing position

alter the depth of your float. The float can be left to travel down at the same pace or it can be held slightly back. Do this by checking the line, leaving the reel with your finger.

When a bite occurs the float will dip under the surface. Trap the line against the reel's spool with your forefinger and strike by moving the rod sideways. As soon as the hook is struck into the fish, close the bail arm of the reel with a quick turn of the reel handle.

When you have hooked a fish, reel in as you bring the rod back into the normal position to play the fish. Do not strike and then suddenly lower the rod as this will slacken the line and could possibly cause the hook to spring out. Keep in contact with the fish at all times. To play the fish towards you, keep the rod tip high and try to steer the fish away from the rest of the shoal without too much disturbance.

As soon as a strike is made, also make sure that the anti-reverse lever on your reel is released, so you can backwind if the fish is large enough to power across into the main current. If you hook a really powerful fish like a barbel, which will swim away from you very quickly, simply release the anti-reverse lever and let the fish take line as it moves off. As the fish slows down you can then begin to apply pressure and play the fish to the awaiting landing-net. Failure to release the anti-reverse lever will result in those first powerful rushes of a fish breaking your line.

When trotting a float down the river the line should be kept fairly straight

reel

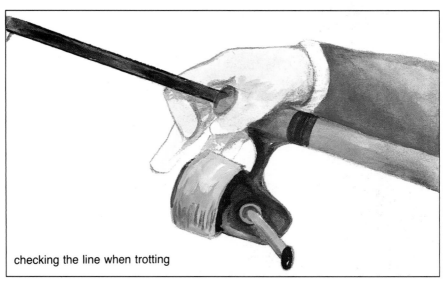

checking the line when trotting

12

throw in loose feed consistently

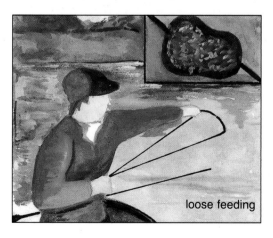

loose feeding

between the rod tip and the float. Sometimes the wind will cause the line lying on the water surface to bow, so this needs straightening. This is known as 'mending the line' and is achieved by rolling the rod tip in a small arc to straighten the line without moving the float out of position. Watch your float at all times.

Leger Tactics

In a fast-flowing river, it is not easy to present a bait acceptable to big fish on float tackle. Barbel and chub will not often chase a bait dragged through at the speed of the current but will accept an offering trundling along the bottom using a rolling leger.

In a flowing river a swim can be explored just as effectively with a leger as it can be with a float. The type of leger which will allow a bait to trundle along a river bed depends a great deal on the nature of the bottom. For example, a

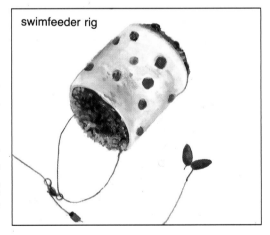

swimfeeder rig

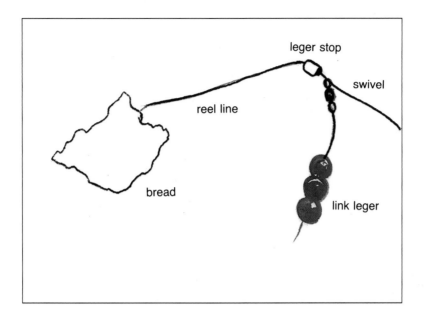

leger stop

swivel

reel line

bread

link leger

drilled bullet is ideal if the bed is sandy. Choose a weight which just holds its position in the current but will begin to roll along as soon as you lift the tip of your rod. Cast across the river and allow your tackle to settle on the river bed. If no bites are forthcoming, raise the rod to set the leger trundling along until it comes to rest again. Hold the rod all the time and touch leger by holding the line between the finger and thumb. In this way it is possible to feel, through the line, the actions of the leger rolling along the river bed. The leger will gradually work down and across the river until it reaches the near-side bank downstream from where you are

fishing. The next cast can be made slightly downstream of the first, searching a fresh area.

On gravelly sections of the river a swan-shot link leger is better than a drilled bullet and will hold bottom easier with less weight.

In a really fast-flowing weedy river, a rolling leger can enable a bait to be presented in places where direct casts are impossible. Fish usually hide away under cover of the waving fronds of streamer weed, and the only way to present a bait to them is to allow the leger to roll under with the force of the current.

Another tactic to use is to quivertip

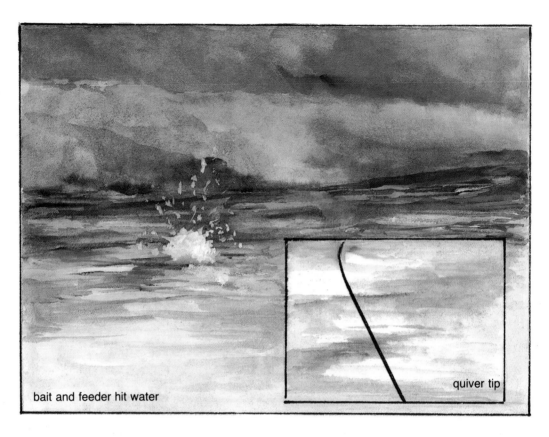

bait and feeder hit water

quiver tip

touch legering

with a swim-feeder rig. If you are fishing the far bank of a river and the current is strong in mid-stream, you can overcome the problem of water pressure affecting the sensitivity of the tip by propping up the rod. This will lift a lot of line clear of the water, thus making the quivertip extremely sensitive and the swim-feeder rig deadly.

Bites can vary a great deal from continuous tweaks and rattles to a full-blooded lunging of the rod. When legering in a heavy current the force of the flow will cause the rod tip to bend

free-line a bait to surface-feeding chub

over. A bite is frequently signalled by the rod tip springing back before lunging forward.

Another tactic is to free-line. In a river free-lining can be a deadly way of catching chub, especially in the shallows. A large knob of cheese paste or a big wad of bread flake moulded round the hook will often be grabbed so violently, as it trundles along the river bed with the current, that the rod is nearly pulled from your hands.

Baits

Anticipation is part of the enjoyment of fishing, and the preparation of baits for a day's fishing greatly enhances this anticipation. Some baits can be bought from your local tackle shop whilst others have to be collected.

Maggot   Without doubt, the most convenient and most widely used bait is the maggot. More than one type of maggot can be bought commercially. The main one used is the larvae of the blow fly; this is used as hookbait. Pinkies and squatts are small so are used as loose feed. Another type is the gozzer which is a good hookbait for bream. To keep maggots at their best, store them in a cool dry place.

Caster   The next stage of the metamorphosis of the maggot before it turns into a fly. They are ideal as a loose feed bait and are often mixed with groundbait. They are also a good hookbait and will produce better-quality fish.

Lobworm   A very good big-fish bait. Take a torch out on a warm evening and walk out onto the lawn. If the ground is moist you will see them lying on the grass. If you are quiet and stealthy you should be able to fill a bait box quickly. They are best kept in damp moss.

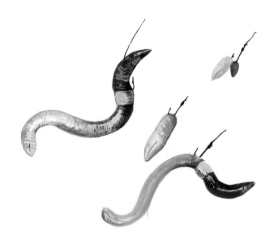

Redworm A very lively worm. A good bait for perch.

Bread A loaf of bread can provide three excellent baits for fishing.

Bread crust A very good bait. It can be used floating on the surface, resting on a submerged weed bed or floating just off the bottom. A bait flavoured by many big fish hunters.

Bread paste Using clean hands, a paste is made by mixing the centre of the loaf with water. Place the mixture in a clean towel and remove any excess moisture. Then knead it until the right consistency is reached. The paste can also be flavoured and coloured during this process. Two good additives are cheese and custard powder.

Bread flake Fresh bread is best suited for this. Pinch out a piece of bread from the middle of the loaf. Squeeze part of it on to the rear end of the hook shank and leave the bread which covers the bend of the hook in its natural state.

Cheese A favourite bait with many anglers as there are so many different sorts. A good bait for many coarse fish.

Sweetcorn A very good bait for roach and chub. An expensive bait but well worth using.

Luncheon meat A great bait for chub and barbel, either float fished or on leger. Please open the tin at home and leave it there, not on the bank side.

Potato Tinned potatoes are a good choice to start with.

Hempseed On a water which is regularly fished with hemp, this is a deadly bait from the start. It is also a very good bait to use as loose feed or mixed in your groundbait. The seed has to be cooked until it splits before it can be used. Ready-cooked hemp can now be bought and this is just as good.

Tares Larger than hemp and needs a little more cooking. It makes a deadly combination when used with hemp and has caused the downfall of many a big roach.

Groundbait A mixture to introduce into the swim you are fishing, or into a swim days before you fish it (this is called 'pre-baiting'). Brown bread-crumbs make a good base, mixed with water. It should have the consistency which allows it to be shaped into balls the size of golf balls; it should not crumble. Samples of baits can be added to the groundbait base – maggots, casters, hemp or sweetcorn, for example.

These balls are introduced by hand or with the aid of a catapult into the swim, where they disintegrate. Heavy groundbaiting can often do more harm than good. Little and often is a more sensible policy.

Knots

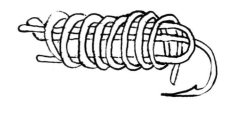

Three-turn Loop knot.

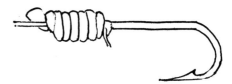

Spade End knot.

Method of joining hook length to reel line.

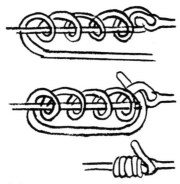

Clinch knot.

Playing and Landing

On hooking a fish, especially a large one, keep the tip of the rod well up and maintain a steady pressure. Never point the rod at the fish. The clutch on the reel must be adjusted prior to fishing so that it yields line when the pressure on it is just below the line's breaking strain.

If a hooked fish makes for an area where underwater snags exist, it can be turned by applying side-strain.

Have the net close at hand. When the fish shows signs of tiring, slip the net into the water and keep it stationary. Never jab at the fish in an attempt to scoop it out. Bring the fish over the awaiting net, not the net to the fish.

Handling and Hook Removal

Always make sure your hands are wet before handling a fish. Grip the fish firmly but gently behind the gill covers. In the case of pike, the jaw will automatically open – don't use gags.

If the hook is slightly embedded near the front of the mouth, it is possible to remove it with the fingertips; otherwise, use a disgorger.

With larger fish, it is best to leave them lying in the damp net while you remove the hook. Artery forceps are best for this. When they are locked, a really good grip is maintained on the hook, which can be gently eased out. A damp towel positioned between the hand and the fish is advisable, as large fish like carp are very strong and need some holding if they suddenly decide to leap about.

Retaining and Returning Fish

Fish should be retained only in a large knotless keepnet, which is well covered by water, preferably in a shaded area. Never keep them for any length of time; in fact, there is no point in retaining them at all unless they are to be

weighed or photographed at the end of your fishing session. Larger fish are best retained in keepsacks where they will lie quietly.

Never throw a fish into a net, but place it gently using wet hands.

When returning fish, gently gather up the net until the area occupied by the fish is reached; place the mouth of the net underwater and allow the fish to swim off.

A large fish should be held underwater in an upright position with both hands until it swims away.

Index